English in Action
Storyteller

Stories to Help You Learn English

by Wally Cirafesi
Illustrations by Toni Summers

English in Action Storyteller: Stories to Help You Learn English
By Wally Cirafesi
Illustrations by Toni Summers

Published by

dawsonmedia

a ministry of The Navigators, P.O. Box 6000, Colorado Springs, CO 80934

The Navigators is an international Christian organization. Jesus Christ gave His followers the Great Commission to go and make disciples (Matthew 28:19). The aim of The Navigators is to help fulfill that commission by multiplying laborers for Christ in every nation.

Dawson Media is a ministry of The Navigators that aims to help Navigator staff and laypeople create and experiment with new ministry tools for personal evangelism and discipleship.

Editor: Leura Jones
Designer: Steve Learned

Printed in the United States of America
ISBN: 0-9672480-8-6

Table of Contents

Acknowledgments

As with the production of any book, *English in Action Storyteller* has been a complete team effort. My wonderful students from Course Design and Materials at Moody Bible Institute were the primary authors of chapters two through twelve, with editing help from Leura Jones and myself. Their contributions were as follows:

Story 2 – A Place to Live (Yrama Kingsley)
Story 3 – A New Language and New Food (Beth Lohmeyer)
Story 4 – A Dream (Sean Gillespie)
Story 5 – Sisters (Nana Lee)
Story 6 – Brothers (Tiffany Claridge)
Story 7 – A Family Reunion (Courtney Camic)
Story 8 – Prejudice (Chris L.)
Story 9 – A Same-Culture Marriage (Julie Koh)
Story 10 – Crossing Cultural Barriers (Anita Crosby)
Story 11 – A Cross-Cultural Marriage (Melissa Dale)
Story 12 – A Generous Employer (Mark Piper)

STORY 1
A Family Move

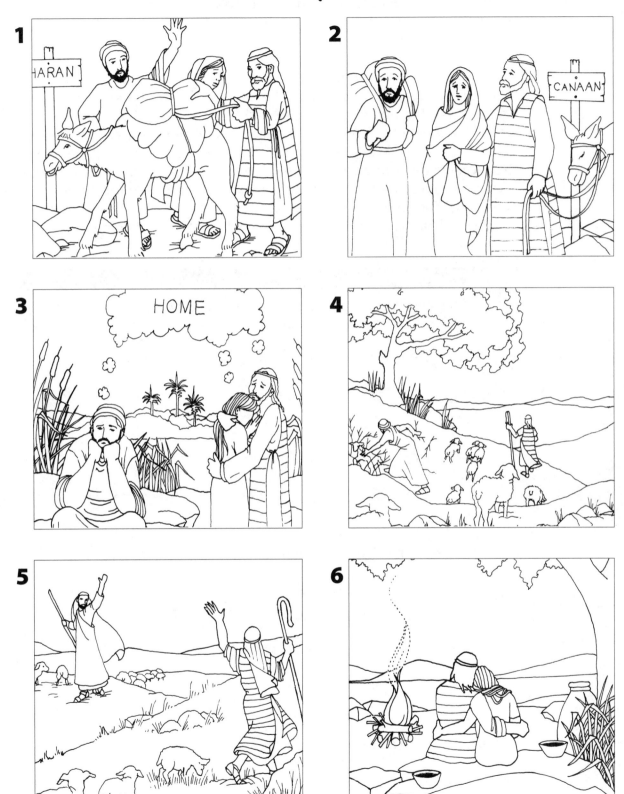

A Family Move

Abram lives in the city of Haran with his wife, Sarai. They're <u>happily</u> married. One day the Lord tells Abram to move his family from Haran to the land of Canaan. Abram's cousin Lot decides to go with them. They <u>gather up</u> all their possessions and say good-bye to their relatives and friends.

It's a long and tiring journey. When they arrive in Canaan, they feel like strangers. The people, the language, the food and even the smells seem different. They feel homesick, but they decide not to think about going back to their home country. They want to <u>make</u> a new life for themselves in Canaan. Abram and Lot own livestock. They work long, hard hours, and their herds grow. They become very successful. Their herds become so large that Abram and Lot decide it would be best for them to separate. Lot thanks his uncle Abram for all of his help and moves to another town. They <u>keep in touch</u>. After years of <u>struggle</u> and hard work, Abram and Sarai finally feel more at home in Canaan.

1 Questions

Write answers to the following questions based on the story. If the story does not answer the question, create your own answer.

A. What do you think the relatives say to Abram and Sarai before they leave Haran?

_____

_____

B. Why do you think Lot decides to go with them?

_____

_____

C. Why is the journey long and tiring?

_____

_____

D. What does it mean to "feel like strangers"?

_____

_____

E. What does it mean to "make a new life"?

_____

_____

F. How do Abram and Lot become successful?

_____

_____

G. Why does Lot move away from Abram?

_____

_____

H. What does it mean to "feel more at home"?

_____

_____

② Vocabulary

Look at the vocabulary words in the context of the story. With a partner, discuss what each word means in context. Then write a true sentence about yourself using the following words from the story.

A. (happily)

_____

_____

B. (gather up)

_____

_____

C. (make)

_____

_____

D. (keep in touch)

_____

_____

E. (struggle)

_____

_____

③ Grammar

Fill in the blanks using the simple past tense of the verbs.

Abram _____ (lives) in the city of Haran with his wife, Sarai.
They _____ (are) happily married. One day the Lord _____
(tells) Abram to move his family from Haran to the land of Canaan. Abram's
cousin Lot _____ (decides) to go with them. They _____
(gather) up all their possessions and _____ (say) good-bye to their
relatives and friends.

It _____ (is) a long and tiring journey. When they _____
(arrive) in Canaan, they _____ (feel) like strangers. The people, the
language, the food and even the smells _____ (seem) different.
They _____ (feel) homesick, but they _____ (decide)
not to think about going back to their home country. They _____ (want)
to make a new life for themselves in Canaan. Abram and Lot _____
(own) livestock. They _____ (work) long, hard hours, and their
herds _____ (grow). They _____ (become) very successful.
Their herds _____ (become) so large that Abram and Lot _____
(decide) it would be best for them to separate. Lot _____ (thanks)
his uncle Abram for all of his help and _____ (moves) to another
town. They _____ (keep) in touch. After years of struggle and hard
work, Abram and Sarai finally _____ (feel) more at home in Canaan.

④ Comprehension

Listen to and then retell each mini-story.

A. Lot is bored living in Haran. He decides to open a booth in the marketplace to sell vegetables. He likes working in the marketplace.

B. One day Abram sees Lot in the market. He tells him that he is planning to move to Canaan, and he invites Lot to join him.

C. Abram's friends try to convince him not to move, but he refuses to change his mind. Sarai also refuses to change her mind about moving.

D. Abram and Sarai used to live next to the open market in Haran. It was always noisy while the market was open. They didn't mind because they were used to the noise.

E. Abram isn't certain how to get to Canaan. He talks to friends and neighbors, but they're not certain either. One day he meets a friend who explains to him the best route to take.

F. When Sarai arrives in Canaan, she has difficulty understanding the people because they speak a different language. She learns to use gestures to make herself understood.

G. Sarai misses shopping at the market back in Haran. The market in Canaan doesn't have many of her favorite vegetables and fruits. She feels disappointed.

H. When Lot moves to a new town, he finds that the people are very immoral. He is upset by their behavior, but he decides to continue living in that town.

I. Abram is looking forward to the future. He knows that God is with him and that he doesn't need to be afraid.

J. Abram and Sarai are so happy. They know the Lord has blessed their lives. They are very grateful, and they pray together often.

Tell this modern story.

1

2

3

4

5

6

6 Writing and Reading

Write one sentence for each drawing in the modern story, or write the story in paragraph form. Then read the story to a partner.

_____

_____

_____

_____

_____

_____

_____

_____

7 Questions

Write a question for the modern story next to each question word.

Example: _Why_ does the young couple move to Chicago?

A. Why?

_____

B. What?

_____

C. Where?

_____

D. How?

_____

E. When?

_____

F. Will?

_____

(8) Your Story

From your own experience or from the lives of relatives and friends, write a story about moving to a new place. Use the following questions and ideas to help you think about what to write.

A. Have you, a relative or a friend moved? When? Why? Where? How?
B. Describe the place you moved from.
C. Describe the place you moved to.
D. How did you feel about the move? Why?
E. Did the food or other things seem strange to you?
F. Did you have to learn a new language?
G. Do you like where you live now?

_____

_____

_____

_____

_____

_____

_____

_____

_____

_____

_____

_____

_____

_____

_____

_____

_____

_____

_____

⑨ Visual Expression

Draw pictures, symbols, shapes or other visual clues to express your story.

⑩ Storytelling

A. Show your drawing to a partner. Allow him or her to ask you questions about it.

B. Try to tell your story by referring only to the drawing.

C. Read your story.

D. Tell the class your story and your partner's story.

A. Groups

   1) Brainstorm together and write a list of things a family needs to do when making a move.

_____

_____

_____

_____

_____

   2) Compare your list with another group.

   3) Decide which three things are the most difficult parts of a family move. List them below.

     a) _____

     b) _____

     c) _____

B. Individually

   1) Fill in the chart.

Three Difficult Things About Moving	Advice on How to Handle This Difficulty
1.	
2.	
3.	

   2) Discuss it with your classmates.

A Place to Live

1

2

3

4

5

6

A Place to Live

One day while Jesus is teaching the people, he tells a <u>brief</u> story. The story is a comparison between two <u>types</u> of people. The story goes like this: There are two men, one called "wise" and another called "foolish." Both of them want to build a new house. The wise man plans the construction of his house very <u>carefully</u>. He knows storms will come someday. He doesn't want the house to collapse during a storm. He decides to build the house on a foundation of rock.

One day a terrible storm does come. It rains <u>really</u> hard and the wind blows. However, the house is strong. It doesn't collapse because it's built on rock. The wise man and his family are safe and secure.

On the contrary, the foolish man doesn't plan the construction of his house very well. He's careless and <u>sloppy</u>. He builds the house on sand; therefore, the foundation is weak. One day a strong storm comes. The rain and wind beat against the house, and it collapses. The foolish man loses everything.

The people understand the meaning of the story: Those who obey Jesus' word are like the man who built his house on the rock.

① Questions

Write answers to the following questions based on the story. If the story does not answer the question, create your own answer.

A. What is the value of telling stories?

_____

_____

B. What does it mean to "plan carefully"?

_____

_____

C. Why does the first man decide to build his house on rock?

_____

_____

D. Why do you think the second man was not as wise?

_____

_____

E. Do you think the foolish man thought about storms? Why or why not?

_____

_____

F. Why is sand not a good foundation for a house?

_____

_____

G. What impact did the wise man's decision have on his children?

_____

_____

H. What advice would you give to the foolish man?

_____

_____

I. What does this story teach us about making decisions?

_____

_____

② Vocabulary

Fill in the blanks with the appropriate word from the story.

brief   types   carefully   really   sloppy

A. There are many _____ of savings accounts.

B. Mr. Ortiz says the meeting is _____ important.

C. A good teacher plans lessons _____.

D. Charlie was very busy, so he made a _____ visit instead of a long one.

E. A lazy worker does _____ work.

3 Grammar

Fill in the blanks using the simple past tense of the verbs.

One day while Jesus _____ (is) teaching the people, he _____ (tells) a brief story. The story _____ (is) a comparison between two types of people. The story _____ (goes) like this: There _____ (are) two men, one called "wise" and another called "foolish." Both of them _____ (want) to build a new house. The wise man _____ (plans) the construction of his house very carefully. He _____ (knows) storms _____ (will) come someday. He _____ (doesn't) want the house to collapse during a storm. He _____ (decides) to build the house on a foundation of rock.

One day a terrible storm _____ (does) come. It _____ (rains) really hard and the wind _____ (blows). However, the house _____ (is) strong. It _____ (doesn't) collapse because it _____ (is) built on rock. The wise man and his family _____ (are) safe and secure.

On the contrary, the foolish man _____ (doesn't) plan the construction of his house very well. He _____ (is) careless and sloppy. He _____ (builds) the house on sand; therefore, the foundation _____ (is) weak. One day a strong storm _____ (comes). The rain and wind _____ (beat) against the house, and it _____ (collapses). The foolish man _____ (loses) everything.

The people _____ (understand) the meaning of the story: Those who obey Jesus' word are like the man who built his house on the rock.

Listen to and then retell each mini-story.

A. The wise man and the foolish man were friends. They moved to a foreign country because life in their own country was difficult. They remained friends even after the storm.

B. The wise man saw a house that was built on a foundation of rock. He wanted to construct one just like it. He worked hard to save his money.

C. The wise man worked very hard for several years to save money. He found a piece of land where he could build his house. Two months later, construction began.

D. Last year there were no hurricanes. However, the wise man knew that sooner or later the storms would come. He was right.

E. The foolish man was a nice guy, but he didn't like to spend money. So he decided to build his house with cheaper materials. Later, he was very sorry that he had used cheap materials.

F. One day the foolish man decides to invite all his friends to his birthday party. A strong storm comes, and the roof begins to leak. His friends get all wet.

G. The wise man invites the foolish man and his family to stay in his house after the storm. They have a nice dinner and a wonderful time together. The foolish man decides to build his next house on a foundation of rock.

H. The wise man was happy because his house was safe and secure. His family was very proud of his decision to build a house with a strong foundation.

I. A good foundation is essential to a sturdy house. A good foundation can help a house withstand storms and even earthquakes.

J. The foolish man was lucky that he survived the storm. He saw that the house was going to collapse, and he and his family escaped to a neighbor's house.

1

2

3

4

5
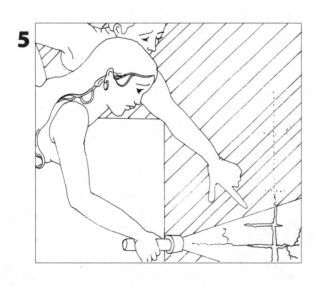

6

⑥ Writing and Reading

Write one sentence for each drawing in the modern story, or write the story in paragraph form. Then read the story to a partner.

_____

_____

_____

_____

_____

_____

⑦ Questions

Write a question for the modern story next to each question word.

Example: *Why* did the couple look at the newspaper?

A. Why?

_____

B. What?

_____

C. Where?

_____

D. How?

_____

E. When?

_____

F. Will?

_____

(8) Your Story

From your own experience or from the lives of relatives or friends, write a story about finding a place to live. Use the following questions to help you think about what to write.

A. Have you ever had to look for a place to live? When? Why? Where?
B. What did you do?
C. Was it difficult to find a place? How long did it take you?
D. What helped you find a place?
E. What do you like about the place where you live?

_____

_____

_____

_____

_____

_____

_____

_____

_____

_____

_____

_____

_____

_____

_____

_____

_____

_____

_____

_____

⑨ Visual Expression

Draw pictures, symbols, shapes or other visual clues to express your story.

⑩ Storytelling

A. Show your drawing to a partner. Allow him or her to ask you questions about it.

B. Try to tell your story by referring only to the drawing.

C. Read your story.

D. Tell the class your story and your partner's story.

(11) Interaction

A. Individually

1) Draw the floor plan of a room you are familiar with. Include windows, doors and furniture.

```
┌─────────────────────────────────────────┐
│                                           │
│                                           │
│                                           │
│                                           │
│                                           │
│                                           │
│                                           │
│                                           │
│                                           │
│                                           │
└─────────────────────────────────────────┘
```

B. Pairs

1) Describe the room to a partner. Include sizes, colors and shapes in your description.

_____

_____

2) Exchange floor plan drawings with your partner. Ask your partner questions about his or her drawing.

_____

_____

3) What questions do you have about finding a place to live?

_____

_____

4) What help do you need to find a place to live?

_____

_____

STORY 3

A New Language and New Food

1 JERUSALEM

2

3 BABYLON

4

5

6

A New Language and New Food

Daniel is a teenager who lives in Jerusalem. He is <u>smart</u> and very handsome. One day, the Babylonian army takes him and others as prisoners. The king of Babylon chooses Daniel to work in his palace. First, Daniel has to learn a new language. He begins to study the language and culture. While in class, he makes three good friends. Their names are Shadrach, Meshach and Abednego.

The king's official tells Daniel and his friends to eat the food given to them. This is a <u>problem</u> because Daniel's religion doesn't allow him to eat certain foods. Daniel feels he shouldn't eat most of the food at the king's table.

He doesn't <u>get upset</u>. He politely <u>explains</u> the problem to the king's official. God helps Daniel so that the official is kind to him and makes an agreement with him. For ten days he and his friends are to eat only vegetables and drink only water. The official wants to see if they <u>look</u> healthy after ten days. After the ten days pass, Daniel and his friends look healthier than everyone else! The official decides that it's OK for them to eat only vegetables and drink only water. Daniel and his friends are extremely happy!

1 Questions

Write answers to the following questions based on the story. If the story does not answer the question, create your own answer.

A. Why does the king choose Daniel to work in his palace?

_____

B. Is language learning easier for Daniel because he is a teenager?

_____

C. Besides the language and food, what additional things may have been new to Daniel in the Babylonian culture?

_____

D. Where does Daniel meet new friends?

_____

E. Why can't Daniel eat the king's food?

_____

F. Why doesn't Daniel get upset?

_____

G. Could Daniel have solved his problem with the food in some other way?

_____

H. What agreement is made between Daniel and the official?

_____

I. Why do you think the official was kind to Daniel?

_____

J. What do you think Daniel learned from this experience?

_____

② Vocabulary

With a partner, discuss the underlined vocabulary words from the story. Write another word in the parentheses to take the place of the underlined word.

A. He is <u>smart</u> and very handsome. (_____)

B. This is a <u>problem</u> because Daniel's religion doesn't allow him to eat certain foods. (_____)

C. He doesn't <u>get upset</u>. (_____)

D. He politely <u>explains</u> the problem to the king's official. (_____)

E. The official wants to see if they <u>look</u> healthy after ten days. (_____)

③ Grammar

Fill in the blanks using an appropriate pronoun.

Daniel is a teenager _____ lives in Jerusalem. _____ is smart and very handsome. One day, the Babylonian army takes _____ and others as prisoners. The king of Babylon chooses Daniel to work in _____ palace. First, Daniel has to learn a new language. _____ begins to study the language and culture. While in class, _____ makes three good friends. _____ names are Shadrach, Meshach and Abednego.

The king's official tells Daniel and _____ friends to eat the food given to _____. This is a problem because Daniel's religion doesn't allow _____ to eat certain foods. Daniel feels _____ shouldn't eat most of the food at the king's table.

_____ doesn't get upset. _____ politely explains the problem to the king's official. God helps Daniel so that the official is kind to _____ and makes an agreement with _____. For ten days _____ and _____ friends are to eat only vegetables and drink only water. The official wants to see if _____ look healthy after ten days. After the ten days pass, Daniel and _____ friends look healthier than _____ else! The official decides that _____ is OK for _____ to eat only vegetables and drink only water. Daniel and _____ friends are extremely happy!

Listen to and then retell each mini-story.

A. Daniel learns the Babylonian language. He becomes very good at his job. Soon the king asks Daniel for advice about government affairs.

B. Daniel worked hard at learning the language. He discovered that learning languages can be fun! It's important to use the language, not just study it.

C. Daniel asks the official for permission to not eat the king's food. The official is scared. If Daniel gets sick, the official will be punished by the king.

D. Daniel doesn't like the food at the king's table. The official puts Daniel in charge of his kitchen to come up with a new menu.

E. Daniel learns the new language very quickly. He likes to practice speaking with people outside of class. He realizes that if he doesn't use the new language, he will never learn it.

F. The king's servants prepare some special Babylonian foods that Daniel can eat. He is afraid to try them at first. He decides to try them. They taste great!

G. Daniel was taken from his family when he was young. His family misses him very much. They wish that they could visit Daniel in Babylon, but that's not possible.

H. Daniel's friends are a great encouragement to him. They "stick with him" in trouble and give him advice when he needs it.

I. Daniel thought of an idea when he was faced with a problem. He was able to please the king's official while still following the rules of his religion.

J. Daniel ended up living the rest of his life in Babylon. He became a trusted advisor and administrator for the king.

Tell this modern story about a girl who travels to a foreign country.

1

2

3

4

5

6

6 Writing and Reading

Write one sentence for each drawing in the modern story, or write the story in paragraph form. Then read the story to a partner.

_____

_____

_____

_____

_____

_____

_____

_____

7 Questions

Write a question for the modern story next to each question word.

Example: _Why_ does the girl look uncertain about the food?

A. Why?

_____

B. What?

_____

C. Where?

_____

D. How?

_____

E. When?

_____

F. Will?

_____

(8) Your Story

From your own experience or from the lives of relatives or friends, write a story about eating new foods. Use the following questions to help you think about what to write.

A. Have you ever eaten food that seemed a little strange to you?
B. When? Where? Why?
C. What was the strange food like?
D. Did you like it? Why or why not?
E. Have you ever had people visit you who thought the food you eat was strange?
F. What should you do if you are asked to eat food that is new to you?

_____

_____

_____

_____

_____

_____

_____

_____

_____

_____

_____

_____

_____

_____

_____

_____

_____

_____

⑨ Visual Expression

Draw pictures, symbols, shapes or other visual clues to express your story.

⑩ Storytelling

A. Show your drawing to a partner. Allow him or her to ask you questions about it.

B. Try to tell your story by referring only to the drawing.

C. Read your story.

D. Tell the class your story and your partner's story.

(11) Interaction

A. Groups

    1) Make a list of the characteristics of a good language learner.

        _____

        _____

        _____

    2) Decide together which two or three characteristics from your list are the most important.

        _____

        _____

        _____

    3) Tell your group what you are doing to learn English.

        _____

        _____

        _____

B. Fill in the blanks below about a popular food dish in your country. Then discuss your answers with your group.

Name of the food:

_____

Description of the food:

_____

When is it traditionally eaten?

_____

Why is this food dish popular?

_____

When was the last time you ate it?

_____

A Dream

1

2

3

4

5

6

A Dream

Joseph is a bright boy, and his father loves him very much. Joseph has a dream that his brothers will one day bow down to him. This dream makes his brothers very angry, so they decide to sell him as a slave.

Joseph ends up in Egypt working for an important official named Potiphar. He does a <u>great</u> job, and Potiphar likes him. One day Joseph is accused of a crime he didn't commit. Potiphar throws Joseph in prison, but even in prison, Joseph works hard and God blesses him.

Two years later, the Pharaoh of Egypt has an <u>unusual</u> dream. He asks his advisors what it means, but no one can tell him. God tells Joseph the meaning of the dream so that Joseph can tell Pharaoh what the dream means. After he explains the dream to Pharaoh, Pharaoh puts Joseph in charge of the <u>entire</u> palace.

Years later, Joseph's brothers come to Pharaoh's palace to beg for food because there is a famine in their homeland. They don't know that Pharaoh's <u>highest</u> official is Joseph, their brother. They don't recognize him. They bow before him to ask for food, and Joseph <u>gives</u> it to them because he loves them. This fulfills the dream that Joseph had as a young boy.

1 Questions

Write answers to the following questions based on the story. If the story does not answer the question, create your own answer.

A. Why didn't Joseph's brothers like him?

_____

_____

B. What did his brothers do to him?

_____

_____

C. Where did Joseph end up working?

_____

_____

D. How well did Joseph do his job?

_____

_____

E. What happened because Joseph was such a good worker?

_____

_____

F. How did Joseph become the head of Pharaoh's palace?

_____

_____

G. Why did Joseph's brothers go to Pharaoh's palace?

_____

_____

H. Why did Joseph give his brothers food?

_____

_____

I. How do you think Joseph's brothers felt at the end of the story?

_____

_____

J. How do you think Joseph felt at the end of the story?

_____

_____

② Vocabulary

The words in Column A are underlined in the story. Match the words in Column B that mean the *opposite* (antonym) of the words in Column A. Place the number next to the vocabulary word.

Column A	Column B
_____ great	1. part of
_____ unusual	2. withholds
_____ entire	3. least important
_____ highest	4. ordinary
_____ gives	5. lowest

③ Grammar

Fill in the blanks using an appropriate pronoun.

Joseph is a bright boy, and _____ father loves _____ very much. Joseph has a dream that _____ brothers will one day bow down to _____. This dream makes _____ brothers very angry, so _____ decide to sell _____ as a slave.

Joseph ends up in Egypt working for an important official named Potiphar. _____ does a great job, and Potiphar likes _____. One day Joseph is accused of a crime _____ didn't commit. Potiphar throws Joseph in prison, but even in prison, Joseph works hard and God blesses _____.

Two years later, the Pharaoh of Egypt has an unusual dream. _____ asks _____ advisors what _____ means, but no _____ can tell _____. God tells Joseph the meaning of the dream so that Joseph can tell Pharaoh what the dream means. After _____ explains the dream to Pharaoh, Pharaoh puts Joseph in charge of the entire palace.

Years later, Joseph's brothers come to Pharaoh's palace to beg for food because there is a famine in their homeland. _____ don't know that Pharaoh's highest official is Joseph, _____ brother. _____ don't recognize _____. _____ bow before _____ to ask for food, and Joseph gives _____ to _____ because _____ loves _____. This fulfills the dream that Joseph had as a young boy.

(4) Comprehension

Listen to and then retell each mini-story.

A. Joseph has a dream. When he wakes up, he can't remember it so he goes back to sleep.

B. Joseph is Jacob's favorite son. Jacob treats Joseph better than his other sons. This makes them jealous. Maybe that's why they sell Joseph as a slave.

C. Joseph's brothers sell him into slavery. They don't want to tell their father the truth, so they tell him that a wild animal killed Joseph.

D. When Joseph goes to prison, he feels upset. He wants to get out, but he decides to work hard and pray instead of getting angry.

E. Joseph has to share a prison cell with two other prisoners. They become friends. One of them gets out of prison, but the other one is put to death.

F. When Pharaoh puts Joseph in charge of his palace, Joseph is amazed. The palace has 75 rooms. It's so big that sometimes he gets lost.

G. When Joseph sees his brothers for the first time in years, he is overwhelmed with emotion. He runs out of the room to cry. After he calms down, he returns to talk to them.

H. When Joseph's brothers recognize him, they are terrified. They think that Joseph must be really angry at them. They can't believe it when Joseph hugs them and says that he loves them.

I. Joseph knew that God was in control of his life. He knew the Lord had placed him in Egypt to help save his family.

J. It took a while for Joseph's brothers to believe that he wasn't angry with them. They felt guilty for the way they had treated him.

Tell this modern story about a woman who dreams of becoming a doctor.

1

2

3

4
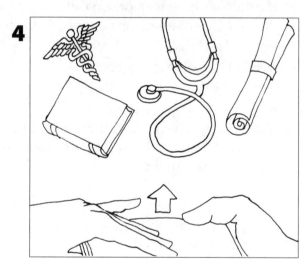

5

6
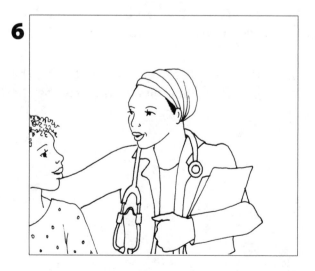

6 Writing and Reading

Write one sentence for each drawing in the modern story, or write the story in paragraph form. Then read the story to a partner.

_____

_____

_____

_____

_____

_____

_____

7 Questions

Write a question for the modern story next to each question word.

Example: _Why_ does the girl study so hard?

A. Why?

_____

B. What?

_____

C. Where?

_____

D. How?

_____

E. When?

_____

F. Will?

_____

⑧ Your Story

From your own experience or from the lives of relatives or friends, write a story about trying to fulfill a dream. Use the following questions to help you think about what to write.

A. What dreams did you have about your future when you were a child?
B. Did you dream about having a particular job or living in a special place?
C. Have your dreams changed since you were a child? How? Why?
D. Do you have aspirations for the future that you think you can achieve?

_____

_____

_____

_____

_____

_____

_____

_____

_____

_____

_____

_____

_____

_____

_____

_____

_____

_____

_____

_____

_____

(9) Visual Expression

Draw pictures, symbols, shapes or other visual clues to express your story.

(10) Storytelling

A. Show your drawing to a partner. Allow him or her to ask you questions about it.

B. Try to tell your story by referring only to the drawing.

C. Read your story.

D. Tell the class your story and your partner's story.

⑪ Interaction

A. Individually, write down the names of the most important "heroes" in your country's history.

    1) Names of heroes from your country:

        _____

    2) Why are these people heroes in your country?

        _____

        _____

        _____

        _____

        _____

        _____

B. Pairs/Groups: Share with your classmates about your country's heroes.

C. Individually

    1) List the five most respected professions (jobs) in your country.

        a) _____

        b) _____

        c) _____

        d) _____

        e) _____

    2) Who is the most admired person in your country right now?

        _____

    3) Discuss your answers with others in the class.

STORY 5
Sisters

Sisters

Mary and Martha are sisters with very different personalities. Martha is <u>outgoing</u>, <u>energetic</u> and always <u>busy</u>. Mary is <u>quiet</u> and likes to sit and talk. They live in a small town. One day, Martha invites Jesus and his friends to have dinner at their house. Immediately, Martha gets busy preparing the meal. She washes plates and cups and dries them. She chops vegetables, bakes bread and prepares meat. She is very worried about getting everything done on time.

In the meantime, Mary is sitting at Jesus' feet and listening to his stories. She enjoys his stories a lot. Martha, on the other hand, doesn't have time to listen to Jesus. She is too busy. She is distracted by all her preparations. Finally, Martha is feeling tired and <u>upset</u>. She wants Mary to help her. She complains to Jesus, "Lord, don't you care that my sister has left me to do the work by myself? Tell her to help me!" Jesus answers her, "Martha, Martha, you are worried and upset about so many things. Mary has chosen what is better, and it will not be taken away from her."

① Questions

Write answers to the following questions based on the story. If the story does not answer the question, create your own answer.

A. How are Mary's and Martha's personalities different?

_____

B. Where do Mary and Martha live?

_____

C. Why does Martha invite Jesus and his friends to her home?

_____

D. Why does Martha prepare a meal for her guests?

_____

E. What does Martha worry about?

_____

F. What does "distracted" mean?

_____

G. What does Martha prepare for dinner?

_____

H. What is Mary doing while Martha keeps herself busy?

_____

I. What is Martha's complaint?

_____

J. Why does Jesus say that listening to him is more important than what Martha is doing?

_____

(2) Vocabulary

Write a true sentence about someone you know using the following words from the story.

A. (outgoing)

_____

_____

B. (energetic)

_____

_____

C. (busy)

_____

_____

D. (quiet)

_____

_____

E. (upset)

_____

_____

3 Grammar

Fill in the blanks using an appropriate preposition.

Mary and Martha are sisters _____ very different personalities. Martha is outgoing, energetic and always busy. Mary is quiet and likes _____ sit and talk. They live _____ a small town. One day, Martha invites Jesus and his friends _____ have dinner _____ their house. Immediately, Martha gets busy preparing the meal. She washes plates and cups and dries them. She chops vegetables, bakes bread and prepares meat. She is very worried _____ getting everything done _____ time.

_____ the meantime, Mary is sitting _____ Jesus' feet and listening _____ his stories. She enjoys his stories a lot. Martha, _____ the other hand, doesn't have time _____ listen _____ Jesus. She is too busy. She is distracted _____ all her preparations. Finally, Martha is feeling tired and upset. She wants Mary _____ help her. She complains _____ Jesus, "Lord, don't you care that my sister has left me _____ do the work _____ myself? Tell her _____ help me!" Jesus answers her, "Martha, Martha, you are worried and upset _____ so many things. Mary has chosen what is better, and it will not be taken away _____ her."

4 Comprehension

Listen to and then retell each mini-story.

A. Mary and Martha are sisters. Martha is a couple of years older than Mary. Mary is a quiet person, but sometimes she argues with Martha.

B. Martha is very responsible and organized. She puts everything in its place. Mary is friendly, but she doesn't like housework.

C. Martha and Mary are at the marketplace shopping for food. The market is very crowded. There's a special sale on vegetables.

D. Mary and Martha's living room is full of guests. Jesus and his twelve followers have come. Everyone is eager to listen to Jesus and ask him questions.

E. Jesus just came back from a long trip. He tells a lot of stories about his trip. Mary asks him a lot of questions.

F. Martha brings food out to the table. It smells delicious. The aroma fills the house, and everyone begins to eat. They compliment Martha on her cooking.

G. There are a lot of leftovers. Martha and Mary put the leftovers in pots and take them to their poor neighbors who need food.

H. Cooking is fun for Martha. She especially likes baking cakes. Her cakes are popular with her neighbors. Every year she bakes different kinds of birthday cakes for her family.

I. Mary and Martha share with each other many different things, including clothes. They are sisters, and sisters should share with each other.

J. Martha is almost like a mother to Mary. She's older and protective of Mary. Despite disagreements, they have a good relationship.

Tell this modern story about sisters.

1

2

3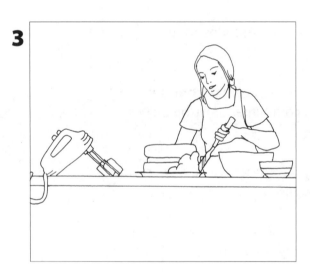

4

5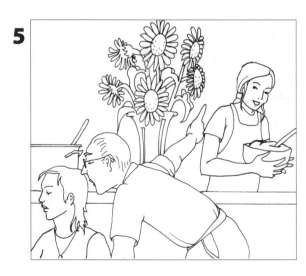

6

⑥ Writing and Reading

Write one sentence for each drawing in the modern story, or write the story in paragraph form. Then read the story to a partner.

_____

_____

_____

_____

_____

_____

_____

_____

⑦ Questions

Write a question for the modern story next to each question word.

Example: *Why* is one of the girls making a cake?

A. Why?

_____

B. What?

_____

C. Where?

_____

D. How?

_____

E. When?

_____

F. Will?

_____

8 Your Story

From your own experience, write a story about a sister, brother, relative or friend who is different from you in personality. Use the following questions and ideas to help you think about what to write.

A. Describe your personality.
B. Describe someone who is different from you.
C. What makes him or her different from you?
D. Are there some ways in which you are the same?
E. Is it easy or hard to get along with him or her?
F. What have you learned about getting along with people who are different from you?

_____
_____
_____
_____
_____
_____
_____
_____
_____
_____
_____
_____
_____
_____
_____
_____
_____
_____
_____

9 Visual Expression

Draw pictures, symbols, shapes or other visual clues to express your story.

10 Storytelling

A. Show your drawing to a partner. Allow him or her to ask you questions about it.

B. Try to tell your story by referring only to the drawing.

C. Read your story.

D. Tell the class your story and your partner's story.

(11) Interaction

A. On the chart below, make a list of chores (responsibilities) that must be done in your home. Indicate who is responsible for each chore and why. For example, who washes the dishes?

Chore	Who does it?	Why that person?
1.		
2.		
3.		
4.		
5.		

B. Interview two classmates. Make a list of chores (responsibilities) from their homes on the chart below. Indicate who is responsible for each chore and why.

Name of Student	Chores in the Home	Who does them?	Why that person?
1.	1.		
	2.		
	3.		
2.	1.		
	2.		
	3.		

C. Share the results of your interviews with the class.

Brothers

1

2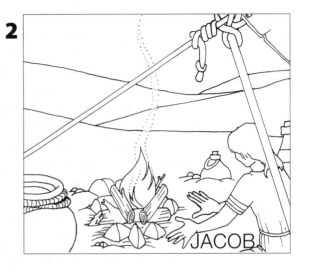

3

4

5

6

Brothers

Esau and Jacob were twin brothers who had different interests. Esau loved the outdoors. As a boy, he used to hunt and fish all the time. Jacob, on the other hand, loved the quiet life and stayed close to home. They constantly competed for their parents' attention and blessing. One day Esau became extremely angry with Jacob. Jacob was so afraid that he decided to run away from home. He went to live with relatives in a place called Paddan Aram.

While Jacob was there, God blessed him with a lot of children and livestock. He became <u>wealthy</u> in his new land. After almost twenty years, Jacob decided to return home. He heard that Esau was coming to meet him, and he was afraid because he thought Esau was still <u>angry</u> with him. He sent a message to Esau as well as a <u>generous</u> gift of livestock. Jacob was hoping the gift would pacify Esau's anger.

Finally the day came when they met. Jacob was feeling very <u>nervous</u>. When Esau saw him, he ran to him and gave him a big hug. He was so happy to see his brother! Jacob was <u>relieved</u> and filled with joy, too. They decided to have a great celebration, and they talked late into the night about how God had blessed their lives.

① Questions

Write answers to the following questions based on the story. If the story does not answer the question, create your own answer.

A. What did the brothers like to do when they were young?

_____

_____

B. What do you suppose that Esau used to do to try to please his parents?

_____

_____

C. What do you think Jacob used to do to try to please his parents?

_____

_____

D. Why do you think Jacob ran away?

_____

_____

E. What do you think Jacob did for a living in Paddan Aram?

_____

_____

F. Why did he wait twenty years to return home?

_____

_____

G. Why do you think Esau was no longer angry at Jacob?

_____

_____

H. Do you think Jacob should have been afraid of Esau after twenty years?

_____

_____

I. What are some things you think Jacob and Esau talked about after not seeing each other for twenty years?

_____

_____

② Vocabulary

Match each vocabulary word from the story with the word that is most closely associated with it. Look at the words in the context of the story. Place the number next to the vocabulary word.

Words from the story	Associated words
_____ wealthy	1. kind
_____ angry	2. comforted
_____ generous	3. worried
_____ nervous	4. rich
_____ relieved	5. upset

③ Grammar

Fill in the blanks using an appropriate preposition.

Esau and Jacob were twin brothers who had different interests. Esau loved the outdoors. As a boy, he used _____ hunt and fish all the time. Jacob, _____ the other hand, loved the quiet life and stayed close _____ home. They constantly competed _____ their parents' attention and blessing. One day Esau became extremely angry _____ Jacob. Jacob was so afraid that he decided _____ run away _____ home. He went _____ live _____ relatives _____ a place called Paddan Aram.

While Jacob was there, God blessed him _____ a lot _____ children and livestock. He became wealthy _____ his new land. After almost twenty years, Jacob decided _____ return home. He heard that Esau was coming _____ meet him, and he was afraid because he thought Esau was still angry _____ him. He sent a message _____ Esau as well as a generous gift _____ livestock. Jacob was hoping the gift would pacify Esau's anger.

Finally the day came when they met. Jacob was feeling very nervous. When Esau saw him, he ran _____ him and gave him a big hug. He was so happy _____ see his brother! Jacob was relieved and filled _____ joy, too. They decided _____ have a great celebration, and they talked late _____ the night _____ how God had blessed their lives.

4 Comprehension

Listen to and then retell each mini-story.

A. Esau goes hunting with his father. They enjoy the outdoors and return home hungry for a hot meal.

B. Jacob breaks Esau's bow and arrows. Esau gets very upset and hits Jacob. Jacob runs to hide in his mother's tent.

C. Jacob leaves home and travels for many days. He feels tired and dirty. He finds a well, takes a drink and sits down to rest.

D. Jacob works very hard at his uncle's house. He takes care of all the livestock. His uncle begins to give him sheep in exchange for his labor.

E. Jacob is in love with Rachel. He wants to marry her. He works for her father so that he will be able to marry her. After a long wait, they finally do get married.

F. Jacob's family is large. He knows he wants to go back to his homeland, so he packs up his belongings and heads for home.

G. Esau is approaching. He is surrounded by many men. Jacob is afraid that Esau will attack him. He prays that God will protect him.

H. Jacob and Esau sit together all day and talk about their lives and families. They couldn't be happier.

I. Jacob felt so good that the bad feelings between his brother and him were now gone. He felt "as light as a feather" in his spirit.

J. Esau's and Jacob's children had a lot of catching up to do. Jacob's children wanted to know all about Grandpa Abraham and Grandma Sarah.

5 Storytelling

Tell this modern story about brothers.

1

2

3

4

5
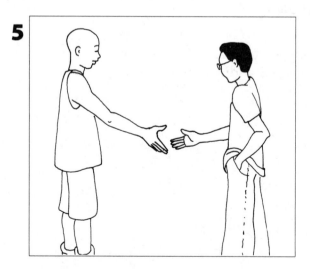

6
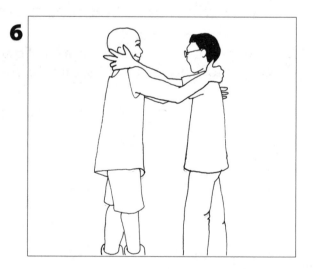

6 Writing and Reading

Write one sentence for each drawing in the modern story, or write the story in paragraph form. Then read the story to a partner.

_____

_____

_____

_____

_____

_____

_____

_____

7 Questions

Write a question for the modern story next to each question word.

Example: *Who* looks like he enjoys being outdoors?

A. Why?

_____

B. What?

_____

C. Where?

_____

D. How?

_____

E. When?

_____

F. Will?

_____

8 Your Story

From your own experience or from the lives of relatives or friends, write a story about an argument. Use the following questions to help you think about what to write.

A. Do you have brothers or sisters?
B. Do you sometimes have arguments?
C. What do you argue about?
D. What do you do when you get in an argument with your siblings?
E. Have you ever been punished by your parents for having an argument?

9 Visual Expression

Draw pictures, symbols, shapes or other visual clues to express your story.

10 Storytelling

A. Show your drawing to a partner. Allow him or her to ask you questions about it.

B. Try to tell your story by referring only to the drawing.

C. Read your story.

D. Tell the class your story and your partner's story.

A. Discuss the following questions with your group.

1) What causes people to have arguments?

_____

_____

_____

_____

2) What have you learned about arguing?

_____

_____

_____

_____

3) What have you learned about resolving conflicts?

_____

_____

_____

_____

B. Discuss together what advice you would give to people who have a disagreement. List your suggestions below.

_____

_____

_____

_____

_____

_____

C. Share your ideas with another group.

A Family Reunion

1

2

3

4

5

6

A Family Reunion

One day the Lord tells Joseph and the king of Egypt that a <u>great</u> famine is coming. They decide to <u>store</u> a lot of Egypt's crops for the future. When the famine comes, Egypt still has plenty of food.

Joseph's <u>extended</u> family is living in Canaan when the famine comes. They <u>run out</u> of food. Joseph finds out that his family is in need and wants to help them. He wants them to come to Egypt so they won't starve to death. He decides to ask the king for assistance, and the king is happy to help. He gives land to Joseph for his family in a place called Goshen.

Joseph sends a message to his father Jacob and tells him to bring the <u>whole</u> family to Egypt. When Jacob receives the message, he is very encouraged. The family starts packing for the journey to Egypt. There isn't much food left. They pack raisins, dates and bread. They have just enough food to make it to Egypt. Once they are packed, they <u>head</u> out on the journey.

Meanwhile, Joseph is very excited that his family is coming. He knows they'll be tired and hungry from the long journey, so he prepares a special meal for them. He hasn't seen his father Jacob for many years. When they arrive, the family has a joyful reunion.

1 Questions

Write answers to the following questions based on the story. If the story does not answer the question, create your own answer.

A. How does the Lord tell Joseph about the famine?

_____

_____

B. Why do Joseph and the king decide to store a lot of crops?

_____

_____

C. Where does Joseph's extended family live?

_____

_____

D. Why does Joseph want his family to move to Egypt?

_____

_____

E. What does the king do to help Joseph's family?

_____

_____

F. Why is Joseph excited?

_____

_____

G. How does Jacob's family travel to Egypt?

_____

_____

H. What happens at the family reunion?

_____

_____

I. How do you think Joseph's family feels after they move to Egypt?

_____

_____

J. What do you think Joseph and his extended family talk about at the reunion?

_____

_____

2 Vocabulary

The underlined words are from the story. Do they have the same meaning in these sentences as they do in the story? Discuss this with a partner.

A. Johnny did a <u>great</u> job.

B. I used to live in an apartment above my uncle's <u>store</u>.

C. The military <u>extended</u> Carmela's leave time.

D. Carrie's parents told her not to <u>run out</u> into the traffic.

E. The decision to close the school was made by the <u>whole</u> staff.

F. Tom hit his <u>head</u> on the low ceiling.

3 Grammar

Fill in the blanks using an appropriate adjective.

One day the Lord tells Joseph and the _____ king of Egypt that a _____ famine is coming. They decide to store a lot of Egypt's crops for the future. When the _____ famine comes, Egypt still has plenty of food.

Joseph's extended family is living in Canaan when the famine comes. They run out of food. Joseph finds out that his family is in _____ need and wants to help them. He wants them to come to Egypt so they won't starve to death. He decides to ask the king for assistance, and the king is _____ to help. He gives _____ land to Joseph for his family in a _____ place called Goshen.

Joseph sends a message to his _____ father Jacob and tells him to bring the whole family to Egypt. When Jacob receives the _____ message, he is very encouraged. The whole family packs their _____ things and heads for Egypt. Joseph is very excited. He hasn't seen his father Jacob for many years. When they arrive, they have a _____ family reunion.

4 Comprehension

Listen to and then retell each mini-story.

A. Canaan used to be green and good for growing many crops. Now the land is completely parched because of a drought. It's losing all of its water, and its trees are dying.

B. The drought eventually leads to a famine because people can't grow crops. Joseph's family couldn't escape the consequences of the drought.

C. Going to see Joseph was like a dream come true for Jacob. He had thought for many years that Joseph was dead. He couldn't believe it when he first heard that Joseph was alive.

D. Joseph's nieces and nephews will be meeting him for the first time. They know he must be a powerful and kind man. They ask Jacob, their grandfather, what Joseph is like.

E. Joseph's brothers are nervous about moving to Egypt. They have to leave their farms behind and find new jobs. They may have to learn a new language.

F. Jacob, Joseph's father, is thankful to God that he will see Joseph again. He puts a special present in his bag to take to Joseph.

G. At the family reunion, everyone hugs each other because they're so happy. Joseph cries when he sees Jacob because he thought he would never see his father again.

H. The family thanks Joseph for inviting them to Egypt. Now they're living in a place that has plenty of food. The family thanks the Lord and sings songs of praise.

I. Goshen is different than Canaan, but Jacob's family adjusts. They know the Lord is with them and will watch over them.

J. Jacob also has the privilege of meeting Joseph's children. He lives for seventeen more years after he moves to Goshen. He thoroughly enjoys being with his son.

Tell this modern story.

1

2

3

4

5

6

6 Writing and Reading

Write one sentence for each drawing in the modern story, or write the story in paragraph form. Then read the story to a partner.

_____

_____

_____

_____

_____

_____

_____

7 Questions

Write a question for the modern story next to each question word.

Example: *Why* are the people hugging?

A. Why?

_____

B. What?

_____

C. Where?

_____

D. How?

_____

E. When?

_____

F. Will?

_____

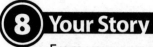

8 Your Story

From your own experience or from the lives of relatives or friends, write your own story about a family reunion or celebration. Use the following questions to help you think about what to write.

A. Have you ever been to a family reunion?
B. Who came?
C. When was it? Where? How often do you have them?
D. Was it fun? What did you do?

_____

_____

_____

_____

_____

_____

_____

_____

_____

_____

_____

_____

_____

_____

_____

_____

_____

_____

_____

_____

_____

_____

⑨ Visual Expression

Draw pictures, symbols, shapes or other visual clues to express your story.

⑩ Storytelling

A. Show your drawing to a partner. Allow him or her to ask you questions about it.

B. Try to tell your story by referring only to the drawing.

C. Read your story.

D. Tell the class your story and your partner's story.

(11) Interaction

A. Individually

1) Think about your family reunions and holiday celebrations to fill out the following chart.

Your Family	1	2	3
Three favorite foods we enjoy			
Three favorite songs, dances or games we like to play			
Three favorite memories I have			

B. Groups

1) Share your answers. Talk about the things that are <u>similar</u> and the things that are <u>different</u> between your families.

C. Individually

1) Remember a time when your family had a special celebration. Write down the jobs that different family members had in helping with the celebration.

Example: Grandfather played music. Grandmother baked bread.

Family Member	Job or Responsibility
Grandparents	
Parents	
Me	
Brother(s)	
Sister(s)	

2) Discuss your answers with your classmates.

Prejudice

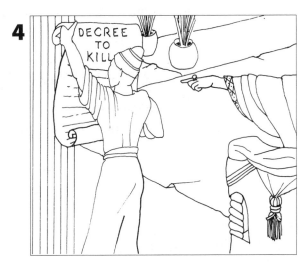

Prejudice

Esther is a young woman who lives with her cousin Mordecai. She is like an <u>adopted</u> daughter to him. Mordecai and his family move to a <u>foreign</u> city. He and his family begin to adjust to their new home. They learn a new language, and they find new jobs. Unfortunately, their new neighbors are not very <u>friendly</u>. They don't like foreigners.

One day the king of the country decides to look for a new queen. He chooses Esther because she is very beautiful. Mordecai can't believe it. Esther is queen! Haman, a deceitful man, works for the king. He hates Mordecai and everyone from his race. He tells the king they're all bad people and that he should get rid of them. The king believes Haman and issues a decree to kill all of them.

Esther hears about this. She is very upset and <u>afraid</u>, but she knows she must do something. She loves her family and wants to help them. Because she is so <u>anxious</u>, she prays for three days. Then she goes into the king's presence to explain the situation. She begs him not to kill her people. The king changes his mind because he trusts Esther and Mordecai. None of her people are killed, and Esther becomes a hero!

① Questions

Write answers to the following questions based on the story. If the story does not answer the question, create your own answer.

A. Why do you think Mordecai adopted Esther?

_____

B. What did Mordecai and his family have to do once they arrived in their new neighborhood?

_____

C. Why were their neighbors unfriendly?

_____

D. How do you think Esther felt when she was selected as the new queen?

_____

E. Why is Haman called a deceitful man?

_____

F. Why does Esther feel like she must do something?

_____

G. What does she do first?

_____

H. Why is she so afraid of going into the king's presence?

_____

I. What causes the king to change his mind?

_____

J. What can we learn from this story?

_____

② Vocabulary

Use the following adjectives from the story in sentences that are true about you or someone else you know.

A. (adopted)

_____

B. (foreign)

_____

C. (friendly)

_____

D. (afraid)

_____

E. (anxious)

_____

Fill in the blanks using an appropriate adjective.

Esther is a young woman who lives with her cousin Mordecai. She is like an adopted daughter to him. Mordecai and his family move to a _____ city. He and his family begin to adjust to their _____ home. They learn a new language, and they find _____ jobs. Unfortunately, their new neighbors are not very friendly. They don't like foreigners.

One day the _____ king of the country decides to look for a _____ new queen. He chooses Esther because she is very beautiful. Mordecai can't believe it. Esther is queen! Haman, a _____ man, works for the king. He hates Mordecai and everyone from his race. He tells the king they're all _____ people and that he should get rid of them. The king believes Haman and issues a _____ decree to kill all of them.

Esther hears about this. She is very upset and afraid, but she knows she must do something. She loves her family and wants to help them. Because she is so _____, she prays for three _____ days. Then she goes into the king's presence to explain the _____ situation. She begs him not to kill her people. The king changes his mind because he trusts Esther and Mordecai. None of her people are killed, and Esther becomes a _____ hero!

(4) Comprehension

Listen to and then retell each mini-story.

A. Mordecai takes Esther back to their homeland for a visit. They meet their old friends and family. After a few days, they return to their new home.

B. Haman sees Mordecai walking. He whispers to his friend how much he hates Mordecai. Mordecai tries to ignore him and keeps walking.

C. Esther cooks dinner for the king and Haman. They enjoy the meal. They tell her that she is a good cook!

D. Haman sees a foreigner on the street. He hurls an insult at him because he hates foreigners. Haman is prejudiced against people who are different from him.

E. One day, Mordecai saves the king's life. The king likes Mordecai for doing this. He gives him a reward, and Mordecai really appreciates it.

F. Esther wants to talk to the king, but she is afraid because it's dangerous to enter the king's presence without his permission. If he gets angry, he could have her killed on the spot.

G. The king listens to Esther. He can tell that she is very upset. He realizes that whatever is on Esther's mind is very important to her. He listens to her attentively.

H. After Esther talks to the king, she is greatly relieved. She tells her servants to spread the word to Mordecai and all the rest of her people.

I. Everyone rejoices at the king's decision. However, the kingdom is so large it takes months for all of the people to receive the new decree.

J. Esther is still considered a hero by Jewish people today. A holiday is celebrated to honor her heroic act. It's called Purim.

Tell this modern story about overcoming prejudice.

1

2

3

4

5

6

6 Writing and Reading

Write one sentence for each drawing in the modern story, or write the story in paragraph form. Then read the story to a partner.

_____

_____

_____

_____

_____

_____

_____

7 Questions

Write a question for the modern story next to each question word.

Example: *Why* is the girl smiling at the end of the story?

A. Why?

_____

B. What?

_____

C. Where?

_____

D. How?

_____

E. When?

_____

F. Will?

_____

(8) Your Story

From your own experience or from the lives of relatives or friends, write a story about prejudice. Use the following questions to help you think about what to write.

A. Have you ever experienced prejudice?
B. How? When? Where? Under what circumstances?
C. How did you respond?
D. Did anyone help you deal with it?
E. Does prejudice exist in your country?

_____

_____

_____

_____

_____

_____

_____

_____

_____

_____

_____

_____

_____

_____

_____

_____

_____

_____

_____

⑨ Visual Expression

Draw pictures, symbols, shapes or other visual clues to express your story.

⑩ Storytelling

A. Show your drawing to a partner. Allow him or her to ask you questions about it.

B. Try to tell your story by referring only to the drawing.

C. Read your story.

D. Tell the class your story and your partner's story.

A. Individually

1) List the qualities of a good neighbor.

a) _____

b) _____

c) _____

d) _____

2) Write the name of a good neighbor you have had.

_____

B. Pairs

1) Discuss your list with a partner.

2) Tell your partner about a good neighbor you have had.

C. Individually

1) Describe your neighborhood in the chart below and then share with the class.

My Neighborhood	Description
Houses	
People	
Stores	
Streets	

A Same-Culture Marriage

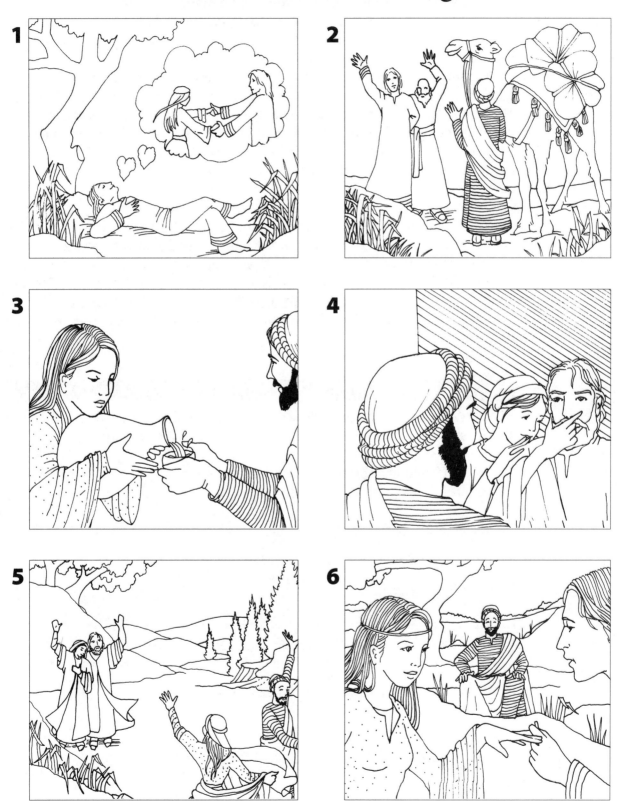

A Same-Culture Marriage

Isaac was a handsome and talented young man. Like other young men, he used to dream about getting married. Abraham, Isaac's father, wanted Isaac to marry a girl from their own culture and language, so he sent his <u>faithful</u> servant back to their homeland to find a wife for Isaac.

The servant chose ten of his master's best camels and loaded them with gifts. He traveled to the small town of Nahor, where relatives of Abraham lived. The servant stopped at a well because he was tired and thirsty. It was early evening, the time when women came to draw water from the well. Rebekah, who was exceptionally <u>beautiful</u> and kind, arrived at the well carrying a water jug on her shoulder. She offered a cool drink to Abraham's servant and his camels.

Abraham's servant sensed right away that Rebekah was the <u>perfect</u> girl for Isaac. Rebekah invited him to meet her family. When he arrived at her home, he gave her family the gifts he had brought with him and explained to them why he had come. After waiting for several days, they gave Rebekah permission to marry Isaac. Soon afterward, Rebekah left home and was on her way to Canaan. She was feeling both <u>excited</u> and <u>anxious</u>. When they arrived in Canaan, she was introduced to Isaac. They fell in love, and not long afterward, they were married.

① Questions

Write answers to the following questions based on the story. If the story does not answer the question, create your own answer.

A. Why do you think Abraham wanted Isaac to marry a girl from the same culture?

_____

B. How do you think the servant felt when Abraham sent him on this trip?

_____

C. Why did the servant go to the town of Nahor?

_____

D. Why do you think the servant carried gifts with him?

_____

E. How did Rebekah show kindness to Abraham's servant?

_____

F. Why do you think Rebekah's family allowed her to leave?

_____

G. What advice would you give to Rebekah?

_____

H. What advice would you give Isaac?

_____

② Vocabulary

The underlined words in the story are adjectives. Change them to adverbs and use each in a sentence.

Example: Robert works in a <u>quiet</u> place. Robert works <u>quietly</u>.

A. (faithful)

_____

_____

B. (beautiful)

_____

_____

C. (perfect)

_____

_____

D. (excited)

_____

_____

E. (anxious)

_____

_____

③ Grammar

Write in the appropriate grammatical article where necessary.

Example: Rebekah was | a beautiful girl.

Isaac was handsome and talented young man. Like other young men, he used to dream about getting married. Abraham, Isaac's father, wanted Isaac to marry girl from their own culture and language, so he sent his loyal servant back to their homeland to find wife for Isaac.

The servant chose ten of his master's best camels and loaded them with gifts. He traveled to small town of Nahor, where relatives of Abraham lived. servant stopped at well because he was feeling tired and thirsty. It was early evening, time when women came to draw water from well. Rebekah, who was exceptionally beautiful and kind, arrived at well carrying water jug on her shoulder. She offered cool drink to Abraham's servant and his camels.

Abraham's servant sensed right away that Rebekah was perfect girl for Isaac. Rebekah invited him to meet her family. When he arrived at her home, he gave her family gifts he had brought with him and explained to them why he had come. After waiting for several days, they gave Rebekah permission to marry Isaac. Soon afterward, Rebekah left home and was on her way to Canaan. She was feeling both excited and anxious. When they arrived in Canaan, she was introduced to Isaac. They fell in love, and not long afterward, they were married.

4 Comprehension

Listen to and then retell each mini-story.

A. Isaac is a good-looking and gifted person. Like most young men, he would like to get married some day. His dad wants him to get married, too.

B. Abraham's servant is not sure how to get to Nahor. He knows Nahor is far away, so he talks to Abraham and begins to carefully plan his trip.

C. Growing up, Isaac used to eat a lot of fruit. Sometimes he used to eat too much fruit and would feel sick. Now he prefers to eat a balanced diet.

D. Abraham's servant was very persistent. He kept going and going until he found a future wife for Isaac. He was the right man for the job.

E. When the servant arrived at Rebekah's house, he was surprised how warmly her family received him. He felt confident then that the family would let Rebekah go with him.

F. The decision to leave was not easy for Rebekah. She loved her family and was a little afraid of going to a new homeland. Once she met Isaac, her fears disappeared.

G. Rebekah always wanted to have a big wedding celebration. She talked to Isaac about her ideas, and he agreed to have a big wedding celebration.

H. Rebekah loves to sing and dance. She sings at family parties. Everyone enjoys listening to her.

I. Abraham is very happy when he meets Rebekah. He knows she and Isaac will be happy together.

J. Abraham and Sarah are getting excited as the wedding day approaches. There are details to take care of and people to invite.

1

2

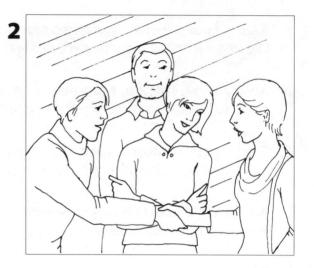

3

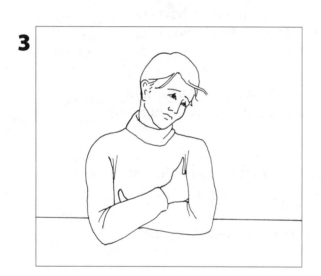

4

5

6

6 Writing and Reading

Write one sentence for each drawing in the modern story, or write the story in paragraph form. Then read the story to a partner.

_____

_____

_____

_____

_____

_____

_____

_____

7 Questions

Write a question for the modern story next to each question word.

Example: *Why* is the young man sad in the third picture?

A. Why?

_____

B. What?

_____

C. Where?

_____

D. How?

_____

E. When?

_____

F. Will?

_____

(8) Your Story

From your own experience or from the lives of relatives or friends, write a story about a "same-culture" marriage. Use the following questions to help you think about what to write.

A. Do young people "date" in your culture? Why or why not?
B. What do parents say about dating and marriage?
C. Are people encouraged to marry someone from the same culture?
D. Do you know someone whose parents arranged his or her marriage?
E. How are weddings performed in your country?
F. What are the customs related to getting married?

_____

_____

_____

_____

_____

_____

_____

_____

_____

_____

_____

_____

_____

_____

_____

_____

_____

_____

_____

_____

_____

⑨ Visual Expression

Draw pictures, symbols, shapes or other visual clues to express your story.

⑩ Storytelling

A. Show your drawing to a partner. Allow him or her to ask you questions about it.

B. Try to tell your story by referring only to the drawing.

C. Read your story.

D. Tell the class your story and your partner's story.

A. Groups

    1) Brainstorm a list of five characteristics of a good husband and a good wife.

Husband	Wife
a.	a.
b.	b.
c.	c.
d.	d.
e.	e.

    2) Discuss your list with another group.

B. Individually

    1) Rank the list of characteristics of a good husband and a good wife in order of their importance to you.

Husband	Wife
a.	a.
b.	b.
c.	c.
d.	d.
e.	e.

C. Groups

    1) Discuss your list and explain your thoughts.

Crossing Cultural Barriers

Crossing Cultural Barriers

Cornelius was a Roman centurion, which means he was responsible for a hundred soldiers. The local community greatly respected him because he loved their nation and was <u>sensitive</u> to the needs of the poor. He often prayed and gave gifts to the poor. One day Cornelius saw a <u>vision</u> of an angel of God. The angel said to him, "God knows that you do good things for the poor." He told Cornelius to invite the Apostle Peter to his home so Peter could tell him about the message of salvation.

So Cornelius sent his servants to find Peter, who was staying at a friend's house in the town of Joppa, near the sea. The servants found the house and invited Peter to go to Cornelius's home. Peter didn't want to go because he knew Cornelius was a Gentile. He had never socialized with Gentiles before. However, the Lord told Peter to go.

The next day he arrived at Cornelius's house. Cornelius was there, along with all of his relatives. They warmly welcomed Peter. This was the first <u>time</u> in his life that Peter had been in the home of a Gentile. He told the people an important lesson he was learning. He said, "God does not <u>show</u> favoritism but accepts men from all nations who <u>fear</u> him and do what is right." Cornelius's family wanted to know about Jesus, so Peter explained the Gospel to them. This was a special day in the life of Peter and Cornelius.

① Questions

Write answers to the following questions based on the story. If the story does not answer the question, create your own answer.

A. Why was Cornelius well respected?

_____

B. Why do you think Cornelius gave to the poor?

_____

C. How did Cornelius's servants find Peter?

_____

D. Why doesn't Peter want to go to Cornelius's house?

_____

E. Why do Cornelius and his relatives greet Peter warmly?

_____

F. What were Cornelius and his relatives expecting from Peter?

_____

G. Why was this Peter's first time in the house of a Gentile?

_____

H. How do you think Peter felt at the end of the day?

_____

I. What important lesson did Peter learn?

_____

J. Why did Peter tell Cornelius's family about Jesus?

_____

② Vocabulary

Read the following sentences. Then write a new sentence in which the underlined word carries a different meaning.

Example: He and his family prayed and often gave to the poor.
New sentence: That was a poor performance by the basketball team.

A. He loved their nation and was sensitive to the needs of the poor.

_____

B. One day Cornelius saw a vision of an angel of God.

_____

C. This was the first time that Peter had been in the home of a Gentile.

_____

D. God does not show favoritism.

_____

E. God accepts men from all nations who fear him and do what is right.

_____

③ Grammar

Write in the appropriate grammatical article where necessary.

          the   the
Example: Cornelius was sensitive to|needs of|poor.

Cornelius was Roman centurion, which means he was responsible for hundred soldiers. local community greatly respected him because he loved their nation and was sensitive to needs of poor. He often prayed and gave gifts to poor. One day Cornelius saw vision of angel of God. angel said to him, "God knows that you do good things for poor." He told Cornelius to invite Apostle Peter to his home so Peter could tell him about message of salvation.

So Cornelius sent his servants to find Peter, who was staying at friend's house in town of Joppa, near sea. servants found house and invited Peter to go to Cornelius's home. Peter didn't want to go because he knew Cornelius was Gentile. He had never socialized with Gentiles before. However, Lord told Peter to go.

next day he arrived at Cornelius's house. Cornelius was there, along with all of his relatives. They warmly welcomed Peter. This was first time in his life that Peter had been in home of Gentile. He told people important lesson he was learning. He said, "God does not show favoritism but accepts men from all nations who fear him and do what is right." Cornelius's family wanted to know about Jesus, so Peter explained Gospel to them. This was special day in life of Peter and Cornelius.

4 Comprehension

Listen to and then retell each mini-story.

A. One day one of Cornelius's servants asks him for money because his daughter is sick. Cornelius is happy to help.

B. The servants look for Peter in Joppa. He is staying at Simon's house. They begin asking people in Joppa where Simon lives. They finally find Peter.

C. Cornelius's servants are going to Joppa. They are looking for Peter. When they find him, he is sleeping. They wake him up and ask him to go with them.

D. The angel of God tells Cornelius to go find Peter. Cornelius doesn't know where Peter lives. He says, "Please tell me where to find Peter."

E. The Lord tells Peter to go with Cornelius's servants. Peter tells the Lord he is afraid to visit strangers. Peter's family encourages him to obey the Lord.

F. Peter invites Cornelius's servants to stay in his friend's house. They eat dinner together. Early the next morning, they begin their journey.

G. Peter leaves his friend's house in Joppa. On the way to Cornelius's house, he meets some friends. They ask Peter if they can go with him. He says yes.

H. Cornelius's house is very large with a patio in the middle. A lot of people can fit into his living room. He invites about forty relatives to come hear Peter speak.

I. Peter tells the Gentiles the special lesson he has learned from God. The Gentiles ask Peter to tell them more about Jesus. Peter is happy to do so.

J. Peter is so excited about what happens in Cornelius's home that he hurries back to Jerusalem to tell his friends. His friends don't believe him at first.

Tell this modern story about two students arriving at college in the United States.

1

2

3

4

5

6

6 Writing and Reading

Write one sentence for each drawing in the modern story, or write the story in paragraph form. Then read the story to a partner.

_____

_____

_____

_____

_____

_____

_____

_____

7 Questions

Write a question for the modern story next to each question word.

Example: *Why* are the boys unpacking?

A. Why?

_____

B. What?

_____

C. Where?

_____

D. How?

_____

E. When?

_____

F. Will?

_____

(8) Your Story

From your own experience or from the lives of relatives or friends, write a story about crossing cultural barriers. Use the following questions to help you think about what to write.

A. Have you ever been to a different culture?
B. Have you ever met someone from a different culture?
C. What are some similarities between you and people who are from a different culture?
D. What are some differences between you and people who are from a different culture?
E. What do you think about the differences? Why?
F. How should you treat someone who is from a different culture?

_____

_____

_____

_____

_____

_____

_____

_____

_____

_____

_____

_____

_____

_____

_____

_____

_____

_____

_____

_____

_____

⑨ Visual Expression

Draw pictures, symbols, shapes or other visual clues to express your story.

⑩ Storytelling

A. Show your drawing to a partner. Allow him or her to ask you questions about it.

B. Try to tell your story by referring only to the drawing.

C. Read your story.

D. Tell the class your story and your partner's story.

A. Groups

    1) Look at the words below and write down other words that come to mind.

        Example: Travel: car, roads, suitcase, planes, distance

        Racism _____

        _____

        Culture _____

        _____

        Neighborhood _____

        _____

        Friendship _____

        _____

    2) Compare your list with those of other groups.

B. Groups

    1) Discuss in your group why racism and prejudice exist.

        _____

        _____

        _____

        _____

    2) Together, list suggestions on how to overcome prejudice and racism.

        _____

        _____

        _____

        _____

        _____

        _____

        _____

A Cross-Cultural Marriage

A Cross-Cultural Marriage

A couple from Judah named Eli and Naomi had two grown sons. One day they moved to Moab because of a famine. <u>Shortly after</u> moving, Eli died. Later, Naomi's two sons married women from Moab. One woman's name was Orpah, and the other woman's name was Ruth. These were cross-cultural marriages. <u>About ten years later</u>, both of the sons also died. Naomi was very upset and didn't know what to do. She decided to return to her home in Judah. Ruth, her daughter-in-law, decided to leave her homeland and return with Naomi. They packed their belongings and moved to Judah.

Ruth began working on a farm. The owner of the farm was a man named Boaz. He was a very honorable man and a relative of Naomi. Ruth worked hard and earned food for herself and her mother-in-law. <u>As time passed</u>, Ruth and Boaz became friends and eventually married. They were from different homelands, but they were willing to have a cross-cultural marriage. Naomi was happy for them. <u>Before long</u>, Ruth gave birth to a beautiful boy named Obed. <u>Many years later</u>, Obed became the father of Jessie and the grandfather of King David.

1 Questions

Write answers to the following questions based on the story. If the story does not answer the question, create your own answer.

A. Why did Eli and Naomi move?

_____

B. If you were Naomi, what would you have taken to Moab?

_____

C. How did Naomi feel after the death of her husband and sons?

_____

D. Why did Naomi return to Judah?

_____

E. How do you think Ruth felt about her relationship with Naomi?

_____

F. How do you think Naomi felt about Ruth returning with her to Judah?

_____

G. Where did Ruth work when she arrived in Judah?

_____

H. What kind of man was Boaz?

_____

I. How did Naomi feel about Ruth's marriage to Boaz?

_____

J. Who is "David," mentioned at the end of the story?

_____

2 Vocabulary

Write a *true* sentence about yourself using the words in parentheses. Write a sentence before that one to give the sentence a context.

Example: I crossed the bridge. <u>Shortly after</u> crossing, the bridge collapsed.

A. (Shortly after)

_____

_____

B. (About ten years later)

_____

_____

C. (As time passed)

_____

_____

D. (Before long)

_____

_____

E. (Many years later)

_____

_____

③ Grammar

Fill in the blanks using an appropriate adverb.

A couple from Judah named Eli and Naomi had two grown sons. One day they _____ moved to Moab because of a famine. _____ after moving, Eli died. Later, Naomi's two sons married women from Moab. One woman's name was Orpah, and the other woman's name was Ruth. These were cross-cultural marriages. About ten years later, both of the sons also _____ died. Naomi was very upset and didn't know what to do. She decided to return to her home in Judah. Ruth, her daughter-in-law, decided to leave her homeland and return with Naomi. They _____ packed their belongings and moved to Judah.

Ruth _____ began working on a farm. The owner of the farm was a man named Boaz. He was a very honorable man and a relative of Naomi. Ruth worked _____ hard and earned food for herself and her mother-in-law. As time _____ passed, Ruth and Boaz became friends and eventually married. They were from different homelands, but they were willing to have a cross-cultural marriage. Naomi was happy for them. Before long, Ruth gave birth to a beautiful boy named Obed. _____, Obed became the father of Jessie and the grandfather of King David.

(4) Comprehension

Listen to and then retell each mini-story.

A. Naomi is packing for the move to Moab. She has many things she can't bring. She leaves them with friends and family. They promise her that they will take care of everything.

B. Eli and Naomi are on the way to Moab. It's a hot day, and they're tired. They stop to eat lunch. They feel better after eating.

C. Eli tries to find work in Judah. He goes to the town square and waits all day, but no one hires him.

D. Naomi is cleaning the house with her daughter-in-law. They clean all day. They're tired, so they will sleep very well tonight.

E. Ruth misses her friends and family in Moab. She writes them a letter. They write back. She's happy to receive a letter from her family.

F. After she arrives in Judah, Ruth receives a message from her mother. She is sick. Ruth hurries back home to help her. She soon recovers from her illness.

G. Boaz is a wealthy farmer. He is able to support Ruth and Naomi very well. They're grateful for his kindness, especially after all of the difficulties they've had.

H. Boaz and Ruth make sure that Naomi lives with them after they get married. They take care of all her needs, and she helps take care of Obed.

I. Obed is a happy baby. Ruth asks Naomi to help her take care of him. Naomi is delighted to do so. She loves to take care of Obed.

J. Obed grows up to be an honest and hardworking husband. He is proud of his son Jessie and his grandson David.

Tell this modern story about a family that has recently arrived in a new country.

1

2

3

4

5

6

6 Writing and Reading

Write one sentence for each drawing in the modern story, or write the story in paragraph form. Then read the story to a partner.

_____

_____

_____

_____

_____

_____

_____

7 Questions

Write a question for the modern story next to each question word.

Example: _Why_ are the man and woman smiling in the third picture?

A. Why?

_____

B. What?

_____

C. Where?

_____

D. How?

_____

E. When?

_____

F. Will?

_____

⑧ Your Story

From your own experience or from the lives of relatives or friends, write a story about marrying someone from a different culture. Use the following questions to help you think about what to write.

A. Are you married to someone from another culture?
B. Have you ever known someone who was married to a person from a different culture?
C. What are the difficulties of a cross-cultural marriage?
D. What are the blessings of a cross-cultural marriage?
E. Are cross-cultural marriages common in your country?

_____

_____

_____

_____

_____

_____

_____

_____

_____

_____

_____

_____

_____

_____

_____

_____

_____

_____

9 Visual Expression

Draw pictures, symbols, shapes or other visual clues to express your story.

10 Storytelling

A. Show your drawing to a partner. Allow him or her to ask you questions about it.

B. Try to tell your story by referring only to the drawing.

C. Read your story.

D. Tell the class your story and your partner's story.

11 Interaction

A. Individually

1) Fill out the following chart. In the characteristic column, choose a word to describe your relative.

Example: Grandpa is "generous."

My Relative	Name	Age	Characteristic
Grandfather (Grandpa)			
Grandmother (Grandma)			
Mother (Mom)			
Father (Dad)			
Brother			
Sister			
Uncle			
Aunt			
Cousin			
Nephew			
Niece			

B. Groups

1) Tell a partner about your extended family. Use the chart to help you.

2) Where does each person live?

3) How often do you see each one?

4) Share a happy family memory that you have.

A Generous Employer

A Generous Employer

One day Jesus told a story about the kingdom of heaven. He explained that the kingdom of heaven is like a farmer who hires people to work in his <u>vineyard</u>. At 6:00 A.M. the farmer travels to the town square to hire <u>workers</u>. When he sees some workers, he offers them a job for the day. They agree to work twelve hours for a day's pay, which is one denarius.

At 9:00 A.M. the farmer returns to the town square to hire more workers. He does the same at noon and at 3:00 P.M. At 5:00 P.M., when there is only one hour left in the workday, he returns again. He finds some more workers, and they go to his fields to work.

At the end of the day, the workers come to receive their pay. The farmer decides to pay the 5:00 P.M. workers first. He gives them a denarius, a <u>full</u> day's pay. When the 6:00 A.M. workers come, they expect to receive more. However, the farmer pays them the same, one denarius. They become very angry. They feel cheated. The farmer says to them, "I didn't cheat you. You agreed to work twelve hours for a day's pay. Are you <u>envious</u> because I am generous? Isn't it OK if I am generous with my own money?" Then Jesus explained the <u>point</u> of the story: In the kingdom of heaven, many who are first will be last, and many who are last will be first.

1 Questions

Write answers to the following questions based on the story. If the story does not answer the question, create your own answer.

A. Why does Jesus tell stories?

_____

B. Why does the farmer go into town four times to hire workers?

_____

C. Why does the farmer hire men to work near the end of the day?

_____

D. Why do some workers feel cheated when they are paid?

_____

E. Was the farmer fair? Explain.

_____

F. How would you describe the farmer?

_____

G. Why are some workers still waiting for a job late in the day?

_____

H. How do you think the 5:00 P.M. workers felt when they were hired?

_____

I. Why did the farmer pay the 5:00 P.M. workers first?

_____

J. What do you think is the point of the story?

_____

② Vocabulary

Look at how each vocabulary word is used in the story. Then write a sentence using a synonym for each word. (A synonym is a word that carries the same meaning.)

Example: (receive)
The workers came to <u>get</u> their pay.

A. (vineyard)

_____

B. (workers)

_____

C. (full)

_____

D. (envious)

_____

E. (point)

_____

Write in the appropriate grammatical article where necessary.

Example: Jesus told|story about|kingdom of heaven.
(a — story, the — kingdom)

One day Jesus told story about kingdom of heaven. He explained that kingdom of heaven is like farmer who hires people to work in his vineyard. At 6:00 A.M. farmer travels to town square to hire workers. When he sees some workers, he offers them job for day. They agree to work twelve hours for day's pay, which is one denarius.

At 9:00 A.M. farmer returns to town square to hire more workers. He does same at noon and at 3:00 P.M. At 5:00 P.M., when there is only one hour left in workday, he returns again. He finds some more workers, and they go to his fields to work.

At end of day, workers come to receive their pay. farmer decides to pay 5:00 P.M. workers first. He gives them denarius, full day's pay. When 6:00 A.M. workers come, they expect to receive more. However, farmer pays them same, one denarius. They become very angry. They feel cheated. farmer says to them, "I didn't cheat you. You agreed to work twelve hours for day's pay. Are you envious because I am generous? Isn't it OK if I am generous with my own money?" Then Jesus explained point of story: In kingdom of heaven, many who are first will be last, and many who are last will be first.

(4) Comprehension

Listen to and then retell each mini-story.

A. Jesus often told stories. Stories sometimes help us understand things about life. Every culture in the world has stories to tell.

B. The farmer got up very early in the morning. He wanted to be at the town square by 6:00 A.M. He left his house at 5:30 A.M.

C. Workers were hired to harvest farm crops. They worked in the hot sun. The men were glad to have a job because a lot of their friends were unemployed.

D. Workers cut hay, picked barley and gathered wheat. Their hands and backs were sore after the long day of labor.

E. In the town square, men were hanging around waiting for a job. They talked about the weather and the latest news in town. Little by little, men began to leave as they were hired to work.

F. The farmer was very generous with his money. He treated and paid his workers well, which was unusual. People wanted to work for him.

G. The workers who felt cheated wanted more money. Instead of being happy that the farmer was generous to the other workers, they were angry.

H. Some workers were paid a day's pay for one hour of work. They were very happy. Those workers spread the word that this farmer was very generous.

I. When the 5:00 P.M. workers arrived home, they told their families what had happened. They couldn't believe it. They had never heard of such a thing.

J. Generosity is a wonderful quality. Jesus is teaching us that God is very generous and is never unjust.

⑤ Storytelling

Tell this modern story about starting a new job.

1
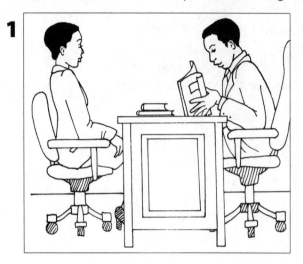

2

3

4
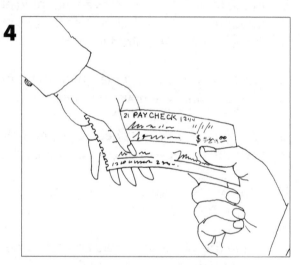

5

6

6 Writing and Reading

Write one sentence for each drawing in the modern story, or write the story in paragraph form. Then read the story to a partner.

_____

_____

_____

_____

_____

_____

_____

7 Questions

Write a question for the modern story next to each question word.

Example: *Why* are the man and woman shaking hands?

A. Why?

_____

B. What?

_____

C. Where?

_____

D. How?

_____

E. When?

_____

F. Will?

_____

(8) Your Story

From your own experience or from the lives of relatives or friends, write a story about work. Use the following questions below to help you think about what to write.

A. Have you ever had a job?
B. How did you find it?
C. What did you do?
D. Do you have a job now?
E. Would you like to have one?
F. What would you like to do?

_____

_____

_____

_____

_____

_____

_____

_____

_____

_____

_____

_____

_____

_____

_____

_____

_____

_____

_____

_____

⑨ Visual Expression

Draw pictures, symbols, shapes or other visual clues to express your story.

⑩ Storytelling

A. Show your drawing to a partner. Allow him or her to ask you questions about it.

B. Try to tell your story by referring only to the drawing.

C. Read your story.

D. Tell the class your story and your partner's story.

A. Groups

   1) List the qualities of a good employer and a good employee.

Good Employer	Good Employee
a.	a.
b.	b.
c.	c.
d.	d.
e.	e.

   2) Compare your list with other groups.

B. Individually

   1) Make a list of the most common difficulties that you experience at work.

     a) _____

     b) _____

     c) _____

     d) _____

C. Groups

   1) Share your list with a partner.

   2) Discuss ways to handle difficulties at work.

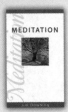